This book is dedicated to my nephew
'Lil' Larry, who transcended this life
but not my heart.

RAISING A
Prodigal
DEVOTIONAL

21-DAYS OF
HOPE AND ENCOURAGEMENT

MARSHA MCLEAN

Studio Griffin
A Publishing Company
www.studiogriffin.net

For information, contact:
Studio Griffin
A Publishing Company
Garner, North Carolina
studiogriffin@outlook.com
www.studiogriffin.net

Cover Design by Ruth E. Griffin
Image by © Anna R/Adobe

First Edition

ISBN-13: 978-1-954818-31-6

Library of Congress Control Number: 2022903441

1 2 3 4 5 6 7 8 9 10

Table of Contents

Introduction

If you've read my book 'Raising A Prodigal: A Story of Encouragement,' you know that my heart is for the prodigal. Having lived it, and watched my son go through it in life, I wanted to help others. That's where my book came from. But I didn't want to stop there. It's possible that as you read my book, uncomfortable and unresolved emotions may come up. That is way I created a workbook ('Raising A Prodigal: Exploration on Your Journey') and now a devotional to support you through this process. Welcome to 'Raising A Prodigal: A Devotional'.

Processing trauma is a complex issue. Regardless of whether you're a Christian or of another faith; whether you're spiritual (or not), a first-time parent, a single parent; whether your child is a straight-A student or a troubled youth; whether you have life figured out or not, we can all use help. I have made it as far as I have because of the help I received along the way. My faith helped me through the tough years of being a single mother and raising a son who challenged my parenting. But it wasn't just my faith. It was also the prayers and advice of others who had already gone through the things I was going through and were now on the other side of it. And that's what this book aims to do—offer help. It's written in twenty-one-day entries. Experts say that if you do something for twenty-one days you've created a new habit and that's that what I want to help you do— create a new habit of seeing hope where you might have felt hopeless before.

The entries are short. I didn't want to give you a whole lot to read. Instead, my goal was to give you nuggets, something to think about as you go about your day. And even though this book differs from the others, my message is still the same: don't give up on your child or whoever your prodigal is. It's okay to feel like a failure sometimes, but don't let that stop you. Everyone makes mistakes but we can learn how to deal with them. Stick in there regardless of what the situation looks like because regardless of what you feel, you aren't alone in this. And most importantly, be encouraged and know the best is yet to be manifest.

Day One

For we are his workmanship, created in Christ Jesus unto good works, which God hath before ordained that we should walk in them.
Ephesians 2:10

God created YOU for this moment. You didn't pick up this book by accident. This moment is where you start new, where you start building a new foundation in your life of love, peace, joy and positivity. Over the next twenty-days, think about what changes you want to make—whether they're for you to help you with a prodigal, someone you love but may be struggling with life. Or for you personally, to help you become a better version of yourself. Know there are somethings you won't be able to change, but at the same time, there are so many others that you can. Focus on those. You have great and wonderful things ahead of you and you are so worth it.

What are three things you would like to get out of this devotional? List them in the space below.

_____

_____

_____

_____

_____

_____

_____

_____

_____

_____

_____

_____

_____

_____

_____

Day Two

A certain man had two sons: And the younger of them said to his father, Father, give me the portion of goods that falleth to me. And he divided unto them his living. And not many days after the younger son gathered all together, and took his journey into a far country, and there wasted his substance with riotous living. And when he had spent all, there arose a mighty famine in that land; and he began to be in want. And he went and joined himself to a citizen of that country; and he sent him into his fields to feed swine. And he would fain have filled his belly with the husks that the swine did eat: and no man gave unto him. And when he came to himself, he said, How many hired servants of my father's have bread enough and to spare, and I perish with hunger! I will arise and go to my father, and will say unto him, Father, I have sinned against heaven, and before thee, And am no more worthy to be called thy son: make me as one of thy hired servants. And he arose, and came to his father.
Luke 15:11-20

This is my favorite Bible story. A loved one left home and lived a life that was beneath him. He lost his way and found himself in a worse place. What I love about this story is that's not where it ended. The son came to himself. He realized that just as he left home, he could go back home.

Home may mean something different to everyone, and sometimes going back to the place and the family you left isn't always the answer. But there is a place you can return to to get revived, to start again and to be successful, regardless of what you've been through. If you've lost your way, go back to that place. And if you know someone who is lost, be that place for them.

What does home mean to you? How can you be home for someone else?

_____

_____

_____

_____

_____

_____

_____

_____

_____

_____

_____

_____

_____

_____

_____

_____

_____

_____

_____

_____

_____

_____

_____

_____

_____

_____

Marsha Mclean

Day Three

But when he was yet a great way off, his father saw him, and had compassion, and ran, and fell on his neck, and kissed him. And the son said unto him, Father, I have sinned against heaven, and in thy sight, and am no more worthy to be called thy son. But the father said to his servants, Bring forth the best robe, and put it on him; and put a ring on his hand, and shoes on his feet: And bring hither the fatted calf, and kill it; and let us eat, and be merry: For this my son was dead, and is alive again; he was lost, and is found.
Luke 15:20-24

Now not only did the son come home, but we see the father was waiting for him. He saw his son from a distance, ran to him and hugged him. It didn't matter that he was gone or that he spent everything he had. His son was back, and he wanted only to celebrate.

When your prodigal returns, celebrate. Love on them. Let them know you appreciate them. That one comfort may stop them from doing something reckless or stupid. The time will come for them to deal with the consequences but until then, celebrate them.

If you have a prodigal in your life, think about the ways that you can celebrate them when they come home. What are some of those ways?

_____

_____

_____

_____

_____

_____

_____

_____

_____

_____

_____

_____

Day Four

The difference between mercy and grace? Mercy gave the prodigal son a second chance. Grace gave him a feast.
Max Lucado

When we talk about mercy and grace, it's often in the same breath, but they are two different things. The son received a second chance at the life he threw away, but he was also celebrated and made a son again. He could have said, "I don't deserve it. I messed up and wasted my life." But the reason for going home, or going back, is to be revived, to start again and to find success. Be open not just to celebrating the prodigal's return, but also to giving second chances. Everyone deserves a second chance.

What are some of the ways you can show mercy to your prodigal? What are some of the ways you can show grace? If you are the prodigal, what kind of mercy and grace would you like?

Marsha Mclean

_____

_____

_____

_____

_____

_____

_____

_____

_____

_____

_____

_____

_____

_____

_____

_____

_____

Day Five

All roads out of hell lead home.
Shannon L. Alder

I've got one more entry for the Prodigal son!

Sometimes the choices the prodigal makes in life turn out to be the wrong ones. They end up taking them down roads they would have never chosen. But there is always another side to it, and if they can find their way out, they can find their way home. That still leaves them with the memory and consequences of the places they left. We can help heal that. If your prodigal has returned home, remember this person has been in a hellish situation: extend some grace. And give them the space they need to heal.

What are some of the things you can do to make home 'home' again for your prodigal? How can you extend grace?

Marsha Mclean

_____

_____

_____

_____

_____

_____

_____

_____

_____

_____

_____

_____

_____

_____

_____

_____

_____

_____

Day Six

*Nothing teaches us about the preciousness of the
Creator as much as when we learn the emptiness
of everything else.*
Charles Spurgeon

Sometimes we get wrapped up in the trivial
things of life. We focus on the materials
things, or the pursuit of a career or what we
think will make us happy. But those are
things that will not satisfy us. Family, friends,
love—that's what truly important in life. And
those are the things that come from God. Be
thankful and appreciate the important things
in your life. When life gets tough, and it will,
focus on the important things and allow them
to help you through those times.

List the top five important things in your life.

_____

_____

_____

Day Seven

Give the ones you love wings to fly, roots to come back and reasons to stay.
Dalai Lama

Part of a being a parent is knowing when to let go and when to help. But that's not always easy, especially when your child is struggling. We can't fix the situation for them, and sometimes we have to actually let them make their own mistakes. But that doesn't mean we leave them do it by themselves. We can encourage them. We can give them advise, especially if we've been through the same thing. And we can always love them. All these things are ways that we help build them up and give them the tools to get through. And it leaves the door open for them to come home.

What are some ways you can help your child(ren) or loved one with something they are struggling with?

Marsha Mclean

_____

_____

_____

_____

_____

_____

_____

_____

_____

_____

_____

_____

_____

_____

_____

_____

_____

Day Eight

Let us all remember this: one cannot proclaim the Gospel of Jesus without the tangible witness of one's life.
Pope Francis

We are all ugly and beautiful at the same time. There may be some things we've done that we're ashamed of; and things we've been through that leave scars we don't like. No one's perfect but that doesn't mean you can't embrace who you are! Because the truth is, there are people out there who can benefit from us doing that. When we can show others that we made it, it can encourage them to keep trying until they make it. So accept who you are and own it. I give you permission!

Write down two things that you've done that can be a witness and a help to someone else.

_____

_____

Marsha Mclean

Day Nine

Every time we open our mouths and speak, we are
either saying let there be light or let there be
darkness.
Glennon Doyle Melton

What are you speaking over yourself? That old saying about words having power is true! Think about what you're saying and how it has been working for you. If you're saying bad things, you probably don't see good things. Start building your foundation today: speak light and positive things over yourself and that will begin to change how you see yourself.

Write down three positive things you can say about yourself every day.

_____

_____

_____

_____

Marsha Mclean

_____

_____

_____

_____

_____

_____

_____

_____

_____

_____

_____

_____

_____

_____

_____

_____

_____

_____

Day Ten

Hold the vision, trust the process.
Unknown

There are many times in life that we just want to skip the bad or challenging times and move ahead to the good times. We don't want to go through the process. But that's when we need to realize that the process has a purpose and that we have to trust it. Yes, the process at times is slow but, hey, Rome was not built in a day! It takes time to build the life you want. Trust the process of building a new foundation of peace, positivity and progress. YES! Say it again: "I am building a new foundation."

What are some of the bad things you wanted to skip? Looking back, how are some of the ways they helped you become who you are?

_____

_____

Marsha Mclean

Day Eleven

Trust in the LORD with all thine heart; and lean
not unto thine own understanding.
Proverbs 3:5

Trust in God. Nothing else needs to be said—
trust in God. Through your pain, through
your journey, and though the times of
silence, trust God. You may not understand
why you're going through what you're going,
but he does. He loves you and he's seen your
end from your beginning. He knows that you
can handle what you're experiencing. He
knows how much stronger you'll be on the
other side of it. Just trust him as you go
through it.

What are some ways you can show God you
trust him? What are some things you can
trust him with?

_____

_____

Marsha Mclean

Day Twelve

*The climb might be tough and challenging, but
the view is worth it.*
Victoria Arlen

You can't always see change right away
when you're trying to make a change in your
life, but if you keep at it, you will. Whatever
you're working at, don't stop. You have
come so far and you're going to make an
impact—not just on your life, but in the lives
of those around you. Keep going. Keep
practicing, even when you don't see the
change you want. You're going to get it. And
it'll have been worth the effort you put into it.

Over the last twelve days, what changes have
you made? Has your insight changed, your
perception been adjusted, and your hope
been revived?

_____

_____

Marsha Mclean

_____

_____

_____

_____

_____

_____

_____

_____

_____

_____

_____

_____

_____

_____

_____

_____

_____

_____

Day Thirteen

H.O.P.E. = Hold On. Pain. Ends.

Pain doesn't last forever. It is part of the process you're going through. All things work for the good of those who love the Lord, and pain in included in that. It may be hard to go through it and it might feel like it won't end, but if you're able to hold onto hope, you'll find the end of your pain. Look up and have hope always.

What are some areas you experience pain? What can you hope for?

_____

_____

_____

_____

_____

_____

Marsha Mclean

_____

_____

_____

_____

_____

_____

_____

_____

_____

_____

_____

_____

_____

_____

_____

_____

_____

Day Fourteen

*Accept yourself, your strengths, your weaknesses,
your truths, and know what tools you have to
fulfill your purpose.*
Steve Maraboli

We sometimes think that it's the big things that will make the biggest changes in our life and help us reach the goals we want to reach. But it's not. What you need to do to perfect yourself is make small improvements: start smiling more, being thankful, showing gratitude, extending grace. These things may not seem as important, especially when we think about our purpose, but when you start with the little things, you start changing who you are on the inside. And as you change that, the bigger things will begin to grow, and be seen on the outside.

List three small things you can start changing today.

Marsha Mclean

_____

_____

_____

_____

_____

_____

_____

_____

_____

_____

_____

_____

_____

_____

_____

_____

_____

_____

_____

What we feel is a choice.
Piyush Shrivastav

Emotions are a gift from God, made to help you navigate your day and the things you go through, but sometimes your emotions are irrational. Sometimes they are out of balance. You can worry or fear too much when there's nothing for you to worry about or fear. You can stay angry and annoyed beyond what is helpful. That's when you need to get out of your emotions. You don't have to stay there with them if they aren't helping you through life. Recognize what you're feeling, then make the choice to change it if that's what you need to do. The choice is yours.

What are some emotions you need to work on changing?

_____

_____

Marsha Mclean

Day Sixteen

*Above all, love each other deeply, because love
covers over a multitude of sins.
I Peter 4:8 (NIV)*

Even when you've been hurt, you can still do
for others what nobody ever did for you!
Regardless of what you went through, you
are still capable of love. Love isn't just an
emotion; it's a choice and you can choose to
love someone back home. You can choose to
love them to a better place. We were made
for each other, and we are at our best when
we love one another. Above all, love.

What are some ways you can show love to
someone who is hurting? How can you love
yourself?

_____

_____

_____

_____

Marsha Mclean

Day Seventeen

*If I wait for someone else to validate my existence,
it will mean that I'm shortchanging myself.*
Zanele Muholi

I want you to understand you don't need any one to validate you. You don't need anyone's opinion when they never had to take your assignments as a parent to your child(ren). Or they never walked in your shoes. Regardless of what you're facing, you are uniquely you and you don't need to wait on anyone to tell you that. Stand in the confidence of who you are, and when you have done all that you can do, continue to stand on that!

Describe who you are, and how you are unique.

_____

_____

_____

_____

Marsha Mclean

_____

_____

_____

_____

_____

_____

_____

_____

_____

_____

_____

_____

_____

_____

_____

_____

_____

_____

Day Eighteen

I learned patience, perseverance, and dedication.
Now I really know myself, and I know my voice.
It's a voice of pain and victory.
Anthony Hamilton

You've heard the saying, "What doesn't kill you makes you stronger." That's what life is about, taking the things that challenge you and allowing those things to help you become better. Turn them around. If you've experienced pain and heartache, allow them to teach you gratitude. If you've lost someone, learn to appreciate the people you have. If someone gave up on you, learn how not to give up on others. Ultimately, the rough parts of life can become the best parts if we learn to look at them as our teachers. And we'll be better because of it.

Think about two times in your life that you were challenged. How did you or can you turn them around?

Marsha Mclean

_____

_____

_____

_____

_____

_____

_____

_____

_____

_____

_____

_____

_____

_____

_____

_____

_____

Day Nineteen

*People, even more than things, have to be
restored, renewed, revived, reclaimed, and
redeemed. Never throw out anyone.*
Audrey Hepburn

Never be tempted to give up on anyone. They
might be reckless and stupid. They might
make decisions that hurt themselves and you.
They might give up on you. But don't give
up. As long as we're still breathing, there is
still hope for revival and renewal. There's still
hope that, like the prodigal son, they might
come home. Love on them, wait for them,
pray for him, hope for them, but don't give
up. Just as you have your own process, so do
they. Focus on the joy you'll feel when they
come home and keep your hope alive.

What can you do while you wait on your
prodigal to return home?

_____

_____

Marsha Mclean

_____

_____

_____

_____

_____

_____

_____

_____

_____

_____

_____

_____

_____

_____

_____

_____

_____

_____

Day Twenty

Now may the Lord of peace himself give you peace at all times in every way. The Lord be with you all.
2 Thessalonians 3:16

We all have our own challenges. But God's desire for us is to have peace to wait, endure and eventually succeed. His presence gives us peace. Find your peace in God, then duplicate it in your situation. That's his desire for us—to have peace in all things in every way. Peace allows you to be stress-free, to endure and feel a sense of security. That way we won't be tempted to give up, or to go back to the things we left behind as a prodigal. Strive for peace.

How can you achieve peace in your life?

_____

_____

_____

Marsha Mclean

Day Twenty-One

Vision without action is merely a dream. Action without vision just passes the time. Vision with action can change the world.
Joel A. Barker

Now that you are twenty-one days in, it's my hope that these nuggets have been able to help you. If you notice, one of the recurring themes in each of the entries was action—you have to do something to get something. You have to act to see change. Change just doesn't happen, you make it so. Peace, joy, rejuvenation—those things require you do something. As you get a vision for where you want your life to do, think about the things that you need to do to make them happen. Seeing and doing go hand-in-hand. And now that you've had the practice and begun this habit, it's my hope that you'll continue it through your life.

List some of the new habits you created since starting this book. What is your vision for yourself?

Marsha Mclean

_____

_____

_____

_____

_____

_____

_____

_____

_____

_____

_____

_____

_____

_____

_____

_____

_____

_____

Conclusion

Thank you for reading this devotional. It is my hope and desire that it has been helpful to you. Continue working on your new habits by going back and reading through your responses. Let them challenge you to continue the work you started. This is your journey—make the best of it, and of yourself!

Marsha Mclean

about The author

Marsha C. McLean is a Licensed Clinical Mental Health Counselor, Licensed Clinical Addiction Specialist, National Speaker, TV Consultant and Author. Marsha has over twenty years of experience in the Mental Health Field. Due to her years of experience and being respected in her field, she helps train new clinicians who reside in North Carolina and Virginia. She has worked in various Human Services Organizations such as NC Department of Corrections, nonprofit organizations, and crisis services. Marsha has worked extensively with the US Military and worked briefly at the US Marine Corp Headquarters. Marsha currently works with a diverse population in her private practice, Revive Therapeutic Services, PLLC.